SCARY BIKERS

John Godber

One of the most performed writers in the English language, John Godber was born in Yorkshire in 1956. A trained teacher with an MA in drama, it was whilst teaching from 1981–83 that he gained national recognition, winning major awards at the National Student Drama Festival and Fringe Firsts at the Edinburgh Festival. In 1984 he was appointed artistic director of Hull Truck Theatre Company. He has written over forty stage plays including *Bouncers, September in the Rain, Happy Jack, Up 'n' Under, Blood, Sweat and Tears, Teechers, Salt of the Earth, Cramp, Happy Families, Gym and Tonic, It Started With a Kiss, Passion Killers, Unleashed, Thick as a Brick, April in Paris, Lucky Sods, On the Piste, On a Night Like This, The Office Party, Losing the Plot* and *Muddy Cows*.

With Jane Thornton he has co-written *Shakers, Lost and Found* and an adaptation of Bram Stoker's *Dracula*. He has also written extensively for television, including *Crown Court, Grange Hill* and *Brookside*, the six-part BBC series *The Ritz* and its sequel *The Continental*, the screenplay *My Kingdom For A Horse* and the film of *Up 'n' Under*. John also devised the BBC series *Chalkface*, and has written the sports documentary *Body and Soul* for Channel Four Television.

Also published and licensed by Josef Weinberger Plays:

BOUNCERS
BOUNCERS (REMIX)
DRACULA (w. Jane Thornton)
LOSING THE PLOT
LOST & FOUND (w. Jane Thornton)
MUDDY COWS
OFFICE PARTY, THE
ON A NIGHT LIKE THIS
ON THE PISTE
SHAKERS (w. Jane Thornton)
SHAKERS RE-STIRRED (w. Jane Thornton)

SCARY BIKERS

by John Godber

JOSEF WEINBERGER PLAYS

LONDON

SCARY BIKERS – Performance edition (April 2019)
First published in 2019
by Josef Weinberger Ltd
12-14 Mortimer Street, London W1T 3JJ
www.josef-weinberger.com / plays@jwmail.co.uk

ISBN: 978 0 85676 379 3

SCARY BIKERS was first performed in a co-production between John Godber Company and Theatre Royal Wakefield in February 2018. Commissioned by Sky Arts 50.

DON .... John Godber

CAROL .... Jane Thornton

JEAN................................. Jane Thornton

ROB .... John Godber

Directed by John Godber and Neil Sissons
Designed by Foxton

CHARACTERS

DON
A hospital porter, redundant miner

CAROL
A former private school teacher

JEAN
A miner's wife, deceased

ROB
An architect, deceased

TIME

The present
(Specific time references in the text should be adjusted accordingly)

ACT ONE

The Set:

A café bar is on stage, with suggestions of the Tour de France decor. The props that are used in the re-telling of how DON *and* CAROL *met are all placed onstage in natural positions, so we do not notice they are props, e.g. coats, helmets, scarves, coats. There is a small bar. At one area, upstage centre, there is a film screen which shows footage of Eddy Merckx talking and winning several Tours de France or Tours de Flanders; this also functions to show footage of roads passing by when the actors are on the tandem which is placed on a plinth in front of the screen. Downstage left is a small stool where a bicycle is being repaired. Further downstage left there is a racing bike, stood upright and held in position by a stand. Off-centre is a large wooden keel and two chairs which serve as the dining area, and over to stage right there is another racing bike held in an upright position by a stand. Both these racing bikes are without chains in order that the pedals will be able to turn.*

House lights fade.

The actor playing DON, *a large man in his mid-sixties, dressed in tracksuit and colourful cycling top, is mending and sweeping the café.* CAROL, *a small woman in her fifties, is about to start clearing the chairs, and then begins to sweep the floor, once* DON *has left the brush by a chair. It is the end of a long day. There is a dustpan and large bin bag stage centre.* CAROL *is attractive and effusive, as she easily converses with* DON, *who does not play the audience.*

"Fleetwood Mac Greatest Hits" plays. Music fades.

CAROL	I was just looking, and it is four; it's four years.
DON	Ar?
CAROL	I thought it was.
DON	That's good, then.

CAROL	Four years today that I opened up.
DON	It soon goes!
CAROL	That's a cause for celebration, then! Glass of wine later.
DON	Life in the fast lane, then!
	(CAROL *considers*.)
CAROL	That means it's nearly eighteen months since we came back from Italy.
DON	Oph!
CAROL	I know!
	(*A beat*.)
DON	Do your legs still ache?
CAROL	They do a bit, actually.
	(*A beat*.)
DON	My behind does!
CAROL	I know what you mean!
	(*A beat*.)
DON	That was a stretch, wasn't it?
CAROL	That was on my bucket list.
DON	It was nearly a kick-the-bucket list, though, wasn't it?
CAROL	It was, wasn't it?
DON	Oh dear!

CAROL	In at the deep end!
DON	That was you!
	(CAROL *moves to sweep up the café.*)
CAROL	Yes, what a holiday that was. I use the term holiday loosely, actually. Oh dear!
DON	Never again!
CAROL	Over a thousand miles.
DON	Oh!
CAROL	Can you remember?
DON	Oh, my legs!
	(*She sweeps and looks at the audience for the first time.* DON *doesn't play the audience.*)
CAROL	Mind you, he still does thirty miles a day, don't you?
DON	Yeah!
CAROL	And then he's at the gym, and he's sixty-five next month!
DON	Yes, I'm looking forward to it!
CAROL	And he's doing an Ironman challenge in June, aren't you?
DON	Apparently!
	(*She sweeps.*)
CAROL	My husband, Rob: only went to the gym to sit in the sauna, but he was cycling mad! (*She sweeps once more.*) All my family have been, but Adam,

	my eldest, doesn't like the idea of Don, and neither does our Carrie, but . . .

DON   And I can understand that.

CAROL   I know, but I've said to them, Don: "He's not replacing your Dad, it's just a bit of company, that's all." Because there's a lot of loneliness about, isn't there?

DON   There is!

           (*A beat.*)

CAROL   I mean, after I lost Rob I didn't feel like meeting anybody. You never think you will. Had no interest, and it's not the same. I mean, it couldn't be! (*She sweeps.*) And I'm as different again to Don's first wife, Jean. Aren't I, Don?

DON   Oh aye, totally different to Jean! Jean was bloody crackers . . .

CAROL   Mind you!

DON   Ye, you have your moments, Carol.

           (*A beat.*)

CAROL   The thing I've learned about Don is, there's no need to exaggerate. (*A beat.*) You know how with some people, they embellish a story, make it more than it actually was? Well you don't have to do that with Don; the truth is bad enough!

DON   Give over!

CAROL   And how we met was a fluke!

DON   Aye, it was!

CAROL	But when it's your second time around, and you're getting on at bit, you have to move fast, don't you?
DON	If you can!
CAROL	And he's got a funny sense of humour.
DON	Yes, I haven't got one!
CAROL	I mean; he even thinks that attacking the Police is funny!
	(DON *stirs slowly.*)
DON	I don't!
CAROL	During the miners' strike . . .
DON	Well that wa' a war!
CAROL	Honestly, with Don, everything goes back to the miners' strike. And all this Brexit stuff!
DON	Oh don't!
CAROL	Are we soft, are we hard?
DON	Ugh!
CAROL	It's all about the miners' strike for him.
DON	Oh don't, honest!
CAROL	No, seriously!
DON	No, don't!
CAROL	I mean I don't agree with him on any of that, because we're chalk and cheese when it comes to Brexit, aren't we, Don?
DON	Yes, I'm t' cheese!

CAROL   But it's the root of all evil, according to him.

DON   Well it was them or uz, wasn't it?

                 (CAROL *sweeps once more.*)

CAROL   I mean, sometimes he sets off on one of his
                 stories and I'm stood there looking at him and I
                 say, "Was that actually true though, Don?" And
                 it turns out it was, so . . . (*A beat.*) I mean him
                 and Jean took the Police on, didn't you?

DON   We did and all!

CAROL   Where was it?

DON   On't old railway sidings at Upton.

CAROL   I mean, Don's a handful, but what must Jean
                 have been like?

DON   Bloody barmy!

CAROL   Some of his stories, honestly . . . I'm either
                 crying my eyes out or laughing my head off! I
                 think that he should be on the stage.

DON   Give over!

CAROL   No, I'm serious!

DON   Give up!

CAROL   Because once you set him off, there's no
                 stopping him.

DON   Cheeky sod!

CAROL   What happened with the Police again, Don?

DON   Oh, don't . . .

CAROL   What was it again? He's got that many!

(DON *begins to pick up the story.*)

DON   Well we'd got nowt to burn, had we, so me and
        Jean went out to get some slack.

CAROL   In the middle of the night, this! Who goes out
        looking for coal in the middle of the night in
        1984?

DON   We did.

CAROL   He did, him and Jean!

        (DON *stands and starts to hold court with the
        audience.*)

DON   It was Jean's fault, to be honest; she couldn't
        keep her mouth shut! We were getting bits
        o' coal from side o't' old railway, and I sense
        somebody wa' looking at uz, but it wa' pitch
        black, and I'm stood there, right . . .

        [LXQ] [SQ]

        (CAROL *becomes* JEAN, *feisty and young.* DON
        *grabs the plastic bag from centre stage and
        they address the audience as a group of
        eight Policemen.* JEAN *is tough, smokes, and is
        uncompromising. She wears a period raincoat. It
        is midnight.*)

        . . . and I've got sack anyway; then Jean says . . .

JEAN   There's somebody there, Don?

DON   I can't see owt, it's pitch black!

JEAN   Are they from round here?

DON   How do I know?

(JEAN *looks into the dark night and can't ignore her findings.*)

JEAN   Are they t' Police?

DON   I don't know if they're in t' Police, do I?

JEAN   Looks like they're t' Police.

DON   Just leave 'em!

JEAN   Are they getting coal?

DON   How do I know?

(JEAN *gets more belligerent.*)

JEAN   Not scared of 'em, are you?

DON   Not one at a time, but if they all came!

(JEAN *calls loudly and aggressively.*)

JEAN   What are you looking at?

DON   Hey up?

(JEAN *calls.*)

JEAN   He'd beat you with double pneumonia!

DON   Bloody hell!

JEAN   They're nicking coal!

DON   So are we?

JEAN   Yes, but it's your job, isn't it?

DON   Not to nick it!

JEAN   I know but it doesn't seem right, what are they gunna do with it, sell it?

DON	I've no idea.
JEAN	Coming up here; nicking our coal and then selling it?
DON	We don't know that though, do we?
JEAN	They're just acting for t' establishment, you know that, don't you?
DON	Listen, I'm not getting into a debate about t' frigging establishment in t' middle of the neet!
JEAN	They're abusing their position, though.
DON	Just keep filling t' sack up!
	(JEAN *shouts to the Police.*)
JEAN	You're nowt but government lackeys!
DON	Bloody hell!
	(JEAN *is more aggressive.*)
JEAN	That's an abuse of privilege, that is, same as it ever was! Nowt ever changes, mate!
DON	Bloody hell, Jean!
JEAN	Hey, you'd better not miss! He'd eat you alive!
DON	Bloody hell! They're probably in the bloody army, they're shipping 'em in from all over!
JEAN	What, to nick our coal? (JEAN *shouts once more at the policemen.*) Come on then, he'll have the bloody lot of you! Yes? Yes! (*A beat.*) Oh shit!
DON	What?
JEAN	They're coming!

(DON *looks up at the audience.*)

DON   Well don't just stand there, get this bag on the
           bike and let's get bloody out of here, you dozy
           sod!

           [LXQ] [SQ]

           (DON *lifts the sack,* JEAN *exits off with it and the
           lights fade to* DON *stood in the café as if nothing
           as happened. The two actors place whatever
           costumes they needed for the scene easily back
           onto various hooks and hangers in the café.*)

DON   Oh dear; Jean, honestly! She'd set a town on
           fire. Couldn't keep her mouth shut!

CAROL   Mind you, me and Rob had some scrapes; we
           once cut four conifers down without getting
           permission. I mean it's not exactly attacking the
           Police, but . . .

DON   I once cut six conifers down, and it wasn't even
           at our house.

CAROL   What have I said, about him? (CAROL
           *recommences sweeping, and puts her dust on
           a shovel.*) I mean he's tough as old boots, but
           when Jean took poorly, he's told me how it
           crucified him. Well it does; that's one thing that
           we do agree on. (*A beat.*) His kids had grown
           up, moved out, been arrested three times,
           according to him, and just when they should've
           been settling down to spend the rest of their
           lives together, Jean wasn't well.

           [LXQ] [SQ]

           (DON *picks up a wheelchair from slightly
           offstage.* CAROL *becomes* JEAN, *in the chair;
           she is clearly not very well. They are central; a
           change of lights depicts a change in location.*

(Don *parks the wheelchair and moves to get a seat from the café and sits beside* Jean, *as LX focus in on that area.*)

DON   Hospitals!

JEAN   What?

DON   Make me feel ill.

               (*A beat.*)

JEAN   This is what we vote for, isn't it?

DON   Is it?

JEAN   'Course it is; we vote to get all best equipment, don't we?

               (*A beat.*)

DON   They're all clowns, though, aren't they?

JEAN   Who are?

DON   Them we vote for.

               (*A beat.*)

JEAN   Well I don't know who you voted for, but I didn't vote for a clown.

DON   Well they're all bloody clowns to me!

JEAN   Well what do you know?

DON   I know they're all clowns, so . . .

JEAN   Oh, shut up!

               (*A beat.*)

DON   Can't keep off the telly.

JEAN   Well that's their job, isn't it?

DON   What, to be on't' telly?

JEAN   Well . . .

DON   Feathering their own nests, most of 'em!

JEAN   They're an organ of the establishment, that's all.

DON   They're only on't' telly because they want to
            sell a book or sommat. Or they want to remind
            a mate they're still alive, so they'll take 'em on
            the board of a bank!

            (A beat.)

JEAN   That's the system, isn't it?

DON   I thought we were all in the system, though?

JEAN   Yes well, we're obviously not in the same
            system as them, are we?

            (A beat.)

DON   Yes, and that's the fault of the system, that is.

            (A beat.)

JEAN   I mean they say one thing and mean a bloody
            other, anyway!

            (A beat.)

DON   Yes, they're like you.

            (A beat.)

JEAN   Well I hope the results of this scan don't do
            that.

DON   You'll be right; never really smoked, have you?

JEAN	Not to call owt.
	(*A beat.*)
DON	I mean, I wouldn't go into politics, anyway!
	(*A beat.*)
JEAN	Well that's a relief because nob'dy would vote for you!
DON	Why wouldn't they?
JEAN	Well I wouldn't.
DON	What, my own wife?
JEAN	No!
DON	Why not?
JEAN	Because if you had your finger on the button you'd be blowing everything to smithereens, for a start. You'd be worse then them in North Korea, you!
DON	How would I?
JEAN	Too hot-headed, can't keep your mouth shut!
DON	Sez you!
JEAN	Sez you!
	(*A beat.*)
DON	And that's what we've got to do, is it, keep our mouths shut?
	(DON *starts to eat an apple; he is vicious the way he attacks it.* JEAN *watches him like he is a lizard.*)

JEAN	'You doing?
DON	'It look like?
	(*A beat.*)
JEAN	Do you have to?
DON	What?
JEAN	It's like being with a gorilla!
DON	What is?
JEAN	How you eat an apple. It's like you're a lizard!
DON	Well what do you want me to do, put it all in, in one go?
JEAN	Well that wouldn't surprise me. Your mouth's big enough.
DON	I've had no breakfast.
JEAN	Do you have to be all over everything?
DON	I'm not all over it!
JEAN	You are!
DON	Well I'm not all over you, am I?
JEAN	You never have been. (*A beat.*) You never have been, really. (*A beat.*) That's another reason nobody would vote for you; if they saw you eating an apple they wouldn't bloody trust you!
DON	Why wouldn't you?
JEAN	You've no respect for food! (*A beat.*) You've been the same for as long as I've known you, you attack everything; t' garden, t' house work, your food, t' postman.

DON	I don't!
JEAN	You do!
DON	I don't attack t' postman!
JEAN	You wa' going to do when he kept cutting through the hedges! (*A beat.*) I mean, why do you have to make such a noise? It's like I can hear your jaw going.
DON	Well I can hear your jaw going now!

(*A beat.*)

JEAN	No wonder you've got indigestion.

(*A beat.*)

DON	I haven't got indigestion!

(*A beat.*)

JEAN	You will have if you keep eating like that!

(*A beat.*)

DON	Well what am I suppose to do, suck it? (*A beat.*) We'd be here all day!

(*A beat.*)

JEAN	We might be here all day anyway, with the length of this queue.

(Don *tries to suck the apple quietly but it just makes her laugh.*)

DON	Is that any better?
JEAN	Don't make me laugh!
DON	Why not?

JEAN	Because it's not funny, that's why!

(A touching moment as both of them understand their potential future.)

DON	Hey we're still here, kid, aren't we?

(A beat.)

JEAN	'Was reading in t' paper, that they haven't got t' proper facilities in here; they're waiting for a new scanner to come. They have to send some to Leeds! (*A beat.*) I say; 2007 and they're sending 'em all the way to Leeds.

DON	They're building a new 'un, though, aren't they?

(JEAN notices she is being called.)

JEAN	Hey, look out; she wants me over there. I've drank that much water, I'm dying for the loo.

DON	Do you need any help?

JEAN	I can walk over there, Don; what do you think I am?

(JEAN struggles to get out of the wheelchair and walk out of the pool of light. DON watches her go and stands holding the wheelchair.)

[LXQ] [SQ]

DON	I was working as a security guard in Ackworth. About a week later Jean called me on my way to work to say t' hospital had been on and we were on a list to go to Cookridge in Leeds to have another scan and see t' consultant. She'd not been at Ponte, coz they'd got a backlog. (*A beat.*) Our Wayne said to go private. (*A beat.*) Heard piss all from our Jeff. Then I got a text to say he wa' in't Maldives and he said to go and

see my MP, to see if I could get further up the waiting list. I wrote, but I never heard owt! (*A beat.*) We finally got to Cookridge about three months later, and Jean had a scan.(*A beat.*) I went in to see t' consultant and she told me that Jean had only got nine months. (*A beat.*) Just like that! (*Silence.*) And then we got in t' car, drove home and I never told Jean what t' consultant had said! I never told her! We just carried on like nowt wa' any different.

(JEAN *re-enters the area* DON *is stood in; she is quite frail and struggles to sit down.* DON *watches the TV and has his work jacket, as he is about to depart for work.* JEAN *sits in the wheelchair.*)

[LXQ] [SQ]

JEAN   What you watching?

DON   Have you heard this rubbish on *Question Time?* They're on about the North, and they don't even live here!

JEAN   I bet they do!

DON   Well I bet that they don't live where we live!

JEAN   Don't watch it if it makes you aggravated.

DON   I'm not aggravated!

JEAN   You bloody are!

DON   What's the point of them sat there fending and proving?

JEAN   Calm down!

DON   I could kick the sodding telly in!

JEAN   Better not, it's a new un!

            (DON *watches TV and references back to* JEAN.)

DON   And every time they're on they have a new suit.
            We're paying for them, you know? And look at
            the bloody colour of that! Who ever told him
            that that suited him?

JEAN   Not you!

DON   Just fending and proving!

JEAN   Why are you watching 'em if it aggravates you?

DON   Because they're on the telly!

JEAN   Well turn it over.

DON   They're on both sides; there's party political
            broadcasts on't' others. They're taking bloody
            over!

JEAN   Calm down!

DON   Why are they even in our house? What are they
            doing in our house, shouting and balling?

JEAN   Yes that's our job, isn't it?

DON   Bloody clowns, all of 'em. They should all wear
            clown outfits! Mind you, that suit that that
            twat's got on looks like a bloody clown's outfit.

JEAN   Aren't you going to work tonight, then, or what?

            (DON *suddenly realises that he is late.*)

DON   Oh bloody hell, look at the time! That's because
            I'm watching these silly sods!

JEAN   You'll get the sack, you will, and then what will
            you do?

(DON *dashes across the stage, picks up a jacket and a small rucksack and sits on one of the stationary bikes. A spotlight picks him out and lights fade as* JEAN *continues to watch television.* DON *pedals the frustration out on his bike, the lights fade on* JEAN *and she eventually exits with the wheelchair during this speech.*)

[LXQ] [SQ]

DON   Ten miles, ten miles just me and the bike, with the rain on my face. And all I could think about was what the consultant had told me; nine months, nine months, she'd said. And we were already on month eleven with the bed downstairs, and I started to think that she'd got it wrong! (*A beat.*) And at work I couldn't stop seeing Jean in the chair, watching them fending and proving on the telly! And I wondered how the hell had Jean ended up like that. Then eight hours later, freewheeling down home . . . (DON *sits up on his bike and relaxes.*) . . . back to my little life, back to my home, that we couldn't swing a cat in! And they were still going at it; on t' wireless, fending and proving, saying that they represented me, and what I was interested in. (*A beat.*) And when I went into where t' bed wa, I saw her; lying on t' top of it. Just laying on top o't' bed. She'd not even managed to get in it! (*A beat.*) After 'undertakers had gone I chucked t' telly through a window!

[LXQ] [SQ]

(DON *drifts upstage, as* CAROL, *wearing the black of a funeral coat, comes with an umbrella downstage. A spotlight picks her out.*)

CAROL   When I lost Rob, I didn't know which way to turn. You don't; one day they're here and then there's just a big gaping nothingness. He said that he wanted to be buried down Carr Lane, near where he'd come from in Upton. (*A beat.*) He'd been one of the grammar school lads, who'd passed his Eleven Plus and gone to Don Valley and then had gone onto university in Newcastle. (*A beat.*) He'd had an architectural practice near York, which is where we lived until he had to let go, when we knew he was ill. (*A beat.*) They're such grey days, aren't they?

[LXQ] [SQ]

(*The light opens up slightly as* DON *enters the scene. He too has flowers and is on his way to* JEAN's *grave.* DON *is his abrupt self, but notices that* CAROL *is upset. The rain drives down; they both act against it.*)

DON   You alright, love?

CAROL   Yes.

DON   You sure?

CAROL   Yes!

(DON *looks at the headstone.*)

DON   Rob Knowles?

CAROL   Yes!

DON   Oh, right. (*A beat.*) Goor, I think he was in t' year below me at junior school.

CAROL   He wanted to come back home.

(*A beat.*)

DON   His dad had a cobblers' shop near t' police station in Upton.

CAROL   Did he?

DON   Blimey, and that's going back. (*A beat.*) What
        wa . . . ?

CAROL   Brain tumour.

        (*A beat.*)

DON   Oph, hell!

CAROL   Yes.

        (*A beat.*)

DON   Well I . . .

        (*A beat.*)

CAROL   They get every penny they deserve, don't they?

DON   Who do?

CAROL   NHS. They were absolutely brilliant with him.

        (*A beat.*)

DON   Hey, tell me about it. I worked in pits, but I'm a
        porter up at Ponte, now, so . . .

        (*A beat.*)

CAROL   Anyway . . .

        (*A beat.*)

DON   I'm sorry for your loss.

CAROL   And yours.

        (*A beat.*)

DON	Aye, they're all in here: my Mam, mi Dad, now mi wife!

(*A beat.*)

CAROL	Well . . . anyway!

(*A beat.*)

DON	And now t' lads I went to school with.

(*A beat.*)

CAROL	Oh dear!

(*A beat.*)

DON	Are you alright? I don't like leaving you if . . .
CAROL	No, no I've got my son at home, so . . .
DON	Aye; I wish I had. (*A beat.*) Anyway! Tek it easy.

(DON *actions to exit the scene, places his funeral clothes upstage and prepares to enter with the wheelchair once more.*)

CAROL	I don't know what Rob would have thought with me stood there crying like a wreck and talking about him to a complete stranger. I mean, don't get me wrong, I'm not a snob, but Rob told me that he couldn't wait to get away. He told me he couldn't bear the small-mindedness of a pit village; but then I think he felt the guilt of being successful, to be honest. (*A beat.*) And I don't know how this sounds, but the funny thing was, when our Adam was injured in a rugby sevens at Pontefract nearly eighteen months later, I saw Don again!

[LXQ] [SQ]

(DON *enters with a wheelchair. He is in Hospital Porter mode.* CAROL *is concerned about her son. Shakes down her brolly, now she is indoors.*)

DON   Nah then; twice in no time!

CAROL   Eh?

DON   I never forget a face.

CAROL   Ah . . . Yes!

           (*A beat.*)

DON   Everything alrate?

CAROL   My son.

DON   Oh hell! Nowt serious, is it?

CAROL   His leg; they think it's a break.

DON   Oph!

           (*A beat.*)

CAROL   Playing rugby!

DON   Oh, I'd have nowt to do with that.

CAROL   There's an open sevens tournament at Pontefract. He only stepped in to fill a gap; he's just up from Oxford.

           (*A beat.*)

DON   He lives down theer, then?

CAROL   He's doing a doctorate at the university.

DON   Oh, right.

           (*A beat.*)

CAROL

I hardly see him as it is, and now this! Last week he came off his bike, and today they think it's a fracture.

(*A beat.*)

DON

Well I hope he's alright.

CAROL

Fingers crossed!

(*A beat.*)

DON

Never fancied rugby; always worried me, putting your head up somebody's arse.

CAROL

Better than putting it up your own, I suppose!

(*A beat.*)

DON

No, it's two wheels for me, allus has been. Eddy Merckx.

CAROL

"The Cannibal"!

DON

Oh right! Fittest man ever, he wa'!

CAROL

Rob was a fan . . . we both did a bit. In fact I opened a cycling café near York about a year ago, in his name, kind of thing.

DON

Oh well, that sounds abhart right!

(*A beat.*)

CAROL

Well anyway!

(*A beat.*)

DON

If I'm ever over that way . . .

CAROL

Yes! Yes! Pop in for a coffee!

DON   Well ar, wi't' Tour de France, in Yorkshire, it's
           massive naar, cycling.

           (A beat.)

CAROL   Busy in here tonight!

DON   This is quiet; you wait while t' pubs turn out.
           It's like t' bloody Alamo in here on a Saturday
           night! Can't move for Cannibals! (A beat.)
           Anyway, if I get up that way on my bike, I'll
           hold you to that coffee. (A beat.) Tek it easy,
           rate, and I hope your lads alrate. (A beat.) Kids,
           eh? Bloody nightmare. I don't see much of mine
           either; there comes a point when it's just you
           on your own, isn't it? Mind you, I don't miss
           mine; rate set of useless getts! (A beat.) See you
           later.

           (DON wheels the wheelchair upstage and
           offstage. CAROL watches DON as he casually
           moves through the hospital as if he owns it.)

           [LXQ] [SQ]

           (CAROL moves upstage and hangs her coat on
           one of the clothes pegs positioned offstage. She
           moves behind the bar and prepares to bring two
           small espressos downstage.)

CAROL   I mean, when I said to, "pop in for a coffee" I
           never actually expected him to! (A beat.) Well
           you don't, do you? Nobody actually takes you
           up on and offer like that, do they? It's just what
           you say to shake somebody off, usually. It's sort
           of a social etiquette. (A beat.) But not with Don,
           on no; one quiet Sunday, who should march
           in here, haul up his bike, and plonk himself
           at the table like he was Sir Bradley Wiggins
           and demand a double espresso? (A beat.) Yes,
           exactly!

[LXQ] [SQ]

(CAROL *brings two coffees down from the bar
area.* DON *enters the space, starts to take off his
cycling helmet and sits at the table.*)

DON   No sugar in mine, thanks.

CAROL   Nice coffee, this.

DON   I'm ready for it!

CAROL   I bet you are!

             (CAROL *sits at the table with* DON.)

DON   Well this is alrate, isn't it?

CAROL   It's not bad, is it?

DON   Aye; nice little spot. Doing well?

CAROL   Not bad. A slow start; a bit radical for some of the
             locals and I've got some teething troubles with
             youths hanging about, but . . . I'm battling on!

DON   You have to!

CAROL   Rob and I had always talked about opening one
             when he retired, but . . .

DON   I can remember him from school; bright lad,
             wasn't he?

CAROL   Oh yes, pretty amazing; well I think . . .

             (*A beat.*)

DON   Yes, I mean, I'd joined a bereavement group for
             about eighteen months after I lost Jean, but I
             was a bit on the young side, like . . .

CAROL   Where was this?

DON	South Kirkby? At The Grove. Nice people, don't get me wrong, but after the fiftieth game of bingo and talk about the strike I'd sort of got it. Hey, I like a rant about the strike, but them lads are hardcore!
CAROL	Really?
DON	Oh, bloody experts! (*A beat.*) They should be on't' telly talking about stuff! Not bits o' kids!
CAROL	Really?
DON	They should have their own channel! Made me realise that we all had a lot in common, though.
CAROL	And what's that?
DON	They hate everybody.

(CAROL *laughs lightly; she gets it*).

CAROL	Well I'm with you on that! Especially after what happened to Rob, and that came from nowhere; it sours your outlook!
DON	I'm serious; dog walkers, car drivers, pedestrians, everybody!

(CAROL *laughs despite herself.*)

Politicians, the police, kids, teenagers, everybody!

CAROL	I know the feeling!

(*A beat.*)

DON	Did you say that you wa' a teacher, then?
CAROL	Well, I wanted to be an artist.
DON	Well what's stopping you?

CAROL   Me!

DON   How come?

CAROL   Well I'm just not good enough, I'm afraid!

               (*A beat.*)

DON   Well I don't know much about art, but that
               could be a drawback.

               (CAROL *is relaxing, and finds his direct charm*
               disarming.)

CAROL   I went to art school in London, but I wasn't cut
               out, so I went to Nottingham.

DON   What, university, like?

CAROL   It was only a teaching training course.

DON   Well I failed all my C.S.E.'s, so . . .

CAROL   Didn't you do O levels?

DON   Not at our school! Lucky if t' teacher turned up!

CAROL   Mind you, I never taught, well not full-time; I
               didn't need to, Rob had his practice, and then
               we had Adam and Carrie, but I don't see much
               of them both; she's at cookery school.

DON   Sounds like a book!

CAROL   So she'll be on the telly soon, I dare say; it's her
               ambition!

DON   I don't watch it.

CAROL   Well I don't watch a lot.

DON   I threw ours through a window! (*A beat.*) No,
               I'm being serious!

(CAROL *sips her coffee.*)

You okay?

CAROL Sorry!

(CAROL *feels guilty at enjoying herself.*)

DON Hey . . . !

CAROL There's not a day that I don't think about him. Everything in here reminds me . . .

(*A beat.*)

DON I know. Hey!

CAROL Sorry.

DON Don't you worry about it!

CAROL Oh dear!

(DON *gets emotional; it's awkward.*)

DON You're bloody setting me off!

CAROL Oh, sorry!

DON Look at us sat here crying!

CAROL Oh, sorry!

DON You have to talk about them.

CAROL I know you do, but people just don't want to know.

(*A beat.*)

DON When I'm on t' bike I always talk to Jean; you know, what should I wear, should I go out, stay in, go away. There's nobody else.

(*A beat.*)

CAROL   What about your kids?

DON   Well they're busy, aren't they, doing what they do!

CAROL   And what do they do?

DON   All sorts!

CAROL   Well that's nice for you, then.

DON   Oh, aye; they keep me on my toes.

           (*A beat.*)

CAROL   Sorry . . . for . . .

DON   Well I didn't expect to come in here and start
           crying, but . . . Oh dear, got me!

           (DON *is fighting back the tears.*)

CAROL   Would you like another, or . . .

           (*It is very awkward.*)

DON   No, I think I'd better . . . otherwise we'll be in
           floods, won't we?

           (DON *stands to depart; it's awkward.*)

CAROL   Getting off, then?

DON   I'd better.

           (*A beat.*)

CAROL   Do you not get away, or . . . ?

DON   Went to Scarborough for a few days last year; a
           bloke at work set me up with a date in a curry

house. The best part of the night was paying for the bill!

(*A beat.*)

CAROL   I should've got my bike and we could've . . .

DON   Yes, that'd've been good!

(*A beat.*)

CAROL   Well we could, if you . . .

DON   What? . . .

CAROL   Me and Rob would . . .

DON   Oh well . . .

CAROL   I mean if you're . . .

DON   Well are you . . .

CAROL   Yes, if . . .

DON   Oh, right!

(*A beat.*)

CAROL   Used to go all over . . .

DON   Listen, I don't want . . .

CAROL   No, honestly.

DON   Well only if . . .

CAROL   We could . . .

DON   If you fancy, but . . .

(*A beat.*)

CAROL   So is that a yes?

              (*A beat.*)

DON   Well that sounds like it could be, doesn't it?

CAROL   So that's that, then!

DON   Well that's that, then! Phew, got that sorted! (*A
              beat.*) I'll give you my mobile number, shall I?
              It's only "pay-as-you-go", so if I don't get back,
              bear with me, rate? I don't always know where I
              am with my limit!

CAROL   So where shall we meet?

DON   Don't ask me; I've never made decision in my
              life. Jean did it all for me. (*A beat.*) In fact I
              don't even know your name, do I?

CAROL   I'm Carol!

DON   Well I'm Don.

CAROL   Nice to meet you, Don!

DON   Nice to meet you, Carol!

              (CAROL *turns to the audience aghast at her
              actions. So does* DON.)

CAROL   I mean, honestly, what was I doing?

DON   What was I doing?

CAROL   I didn't know anything about him!

DON   And I didn't know owt about her, did I?

CAROL   Except for the fact that he was a hospital porter.

DON   Except that she wanted to be an artist but she
              wa' shit at art!

CAROL	And the crazy thing was, two weeks later we were re-running the Tour de Yorkshire all over Tadcaster.
DON	Yes, but at half the speed!
	[LXQ] [SQ]
	(CAROL *and* DON *reach for helmets and glasses and mount the bikes on either side of the stage. Spotlights and dappled gobos pick these out. It is hard graft.*)
CAROL	These hills are good!
DON	We can stop if you want!
CAROL	Downhill is easier, have you noticed?
DON	Yes, I've noticed that!
	(*A beat.*)
CAROL	At least Adam's got back to Oxford.
DON	That's good, then!
CAROL	But he can't go anywhere near a rugby ball for nine months!
DON	What's it like down there, then?
CAROL	Very nice!
DON	Never been.
CAROL	There's a lot of students on bikes who think the world owes them a living.
DON	Toffs, are they?
CAROL	Some are; not all of 'em.

DON   The establishment?

CAROL   Sounds sinister, doesn't it?

DON   It might be, for all I know!

CAROL   Born to rule, Rob used to say.

DON   That's scary!

CAROL   Absolutely!

             (*They pedal on.*)

DON   What's he studying?

CAROL   He did PPE.

DON   PE?

CAROL   Eh?

DON   What did you say?

CAROL   PPE.

DON   What's that, then?

CAROL   Politics. Philosophy. Economics. He's doing a
             research degree now.

DON   Oh, bloody hell!

CAROL   He wants to change the world.

DON   Well somebody needs to.

             (*They pedal on.*)

CAROL   What do you think about Cameron and the
             referendum, then?

DON   He reckons we'll stay in, doesn't he?

(*A beat.*)

CAROL   I thought you'd've had more to say than that.

DON   I'm on my best behaviour though, aren't I?

          (*They pedal on.*)

CAROL   What's the furthest you've ever gone on a bike, then?

DON   A hundred miles in a day.

CAROL   When was that?

DON   Last week when I came up here for that coffee!

CAROL   Really?

          (*A beat.*)

DON   And I couldn't stand up straight that night; my bloody back and knees had gone!

          (CAROL *and* DON *begin to pedal as if they have just hit a very steep hill; they stand and the effort is deeply felt as they struggle against the incline. Then they are flatter and they call to each other across the stage, and we get the sense that their efforts are less through the strain in their voices.*)

CAROL   This is better!

          (*They pedal easier.*)

DON   So what have you got planned, then? Any holidays, or . . . ?

CAROL   Well I've made myself a bucket list!

DON   A bucket what?

CAROL	The kids think that I'm losing it, but . . . a bucket list!
DON	What's that, then?
CAROL	I'm planning to go to Florence!
DON	Not on a bike?
CAROL	Yes!
DON	How far is that, then?
CAROL	Too far, but you take a train between the major cities.
DON	Oh, that's cheating!
CAROL	Well it's eighty miles a day from Paris to Geneva! Then a train to Pisa, then it's thirty miles a day to Florence.

(*They pedal easily, calling to each other.*)

	Paris to Geneva was set up after the Grand Depart by some business friends of Rob's who he used to go cycling with, and Pisa to Florence is just a bit of fun!
DON	How do you get to Paris, then?
CAROL	Ferry to Zeebrugge, then down to Oudenaarde, overnight in Ghent, then a train to Paris.
DON	Bloody hell, how much is it?
CAROL	Just over two grand.
DON	What?
CAROL	That's not bad!
DON	Oh!

(*A beat.*)

CAROL   Wouldn't you fancy the challenge?

DON   The price is the challenge!

(*A beat.*)

CAROL   You never been to Italy?

DON   We were going to go to the Amalfi coast but Jean wasn't so good, so . . .

CAROL   Well if you fancy seeing Florence . . .

(*A beat.*)

DON   Well, I wouldn't pay that!

CAROL   All your food's in, so . . .

DON   No way!

CAROL   And the accommodation.

DON   No chance!

CAROL   Well let me know. You could always owe me, if you fancy . . .

(CAROL *and* DON *action to stop pedalling.* DON *dismounts from his bike. They face each other from their respective sides of the stage as the state opens up slightly.*)

DON   Wow, hang on . . .

CAROL   What?

DON   Wow . . .

CAROL   Why, what . . . ?

DON	Two grand, bloody hell!
	(*A beat.*)
CAROL	Sorry, I shouldn't've assumed . . .
DON	I mean . . .
CAROL	I didn't mean to offend you.
DON	You haven't offended me, I just can't afford it!
	(*A beat.*)
CAROL	I just thought I'd mention it.
	(*A beat.*)
DON	Is that what you'd expect to pay, then?
CAROL	Well it's an all-inclusive for two and a half weeks in June. What with the transportation and the hotels and that.
DON	Bloody hell!
CAROL	It's not that bad, really . . .
DON	Can you not camp?
CAROL	Camp?
DON	Well aye!
CAROL	Who am I, Tarzan?
DON	Well, I know, but . . .
CAROL	Don, I'm nearly sixty; sad to say it out loud, but . . .
DON	Well I'm nearer seventy, so . . .

(*A beat.*)

CAROL   I shouldn't have mentioned it . . .

DON   No, I er . . .

CAROL   Sorry!

                (*A beat.*)

DON   I mean, it sounds great . . . but . . . (*A beat.*) . . . that's a bit out of my league!

CAROL   Tell you what, come on; shall we race to the farm on the corner?

                (CAROL *begins to cycle as if she is pulling away.*)

DON   Well you've got a bloody head start, haven't you? Story o' my life, that!

                [LXQ] [SQ]

                (DON *exits as* CAROL *turns to the audience, and continues to pedal and speak to the audience. LX fades on* DON's *bike.*)

CAROL   I mean, why not? That's what I said to myself; why not? What was so wrong with me asking him? If you don't ask you never get! I'd spent a lifetime telling my kids that! (*A beat.*) But I felt so bloody awful, putting him on the spot! Assuming he could just magic two grand out of mid-air, like I could. (CAROL *stops pedalling, steps from the bike and begins to take off her helmet and windjammer.*) And goodness knows what Rob would have said if he'd have heard that I had asked a man I hardly knew to come to Florence with me on a bike ride. He'd have probably said . . .

                [LXQ] [SQ]

(DON *enters wearing a large, smart, black coat, and a pair of trendy glasses. He is* ROB *incarnate; he has a briefcase and some architects' drawings. Posh, but likeable.* ROB *is caught in a spotlight.*)

ROB	What?
CAROL	I know, I shouldn't've had said it!
ROB	So, why did you?
CAROL	It's difficult! You know, meeting people.
ROB	Well it is a bit early to be thinking about that anyway, isn't it?
CAROL	Is it?
ROB	I don't know, is it?

(*A beat.*)

CAROL	Well, apparently you went to school with him, so . . .
ROB	That was a million years ago! What's he called again?
CAROL	Don!
ROB	Don what?
CAROL	I don't know! Don something.

(*A beat.*)

ROB	Well it's obviously Don something, isn't it? What is it, Don Smith, or Don Maclean, or Don Revie? What is it, Donna Summer?
CAROL	Funny!

ROB	I mean he looks like an armed robber, for a start!
	(There is real affection between these two worlds.)
CAROL	Well you were no oil painting, were you?
	(A beat.)
ROB	Well with the bloody stress I was under with all the reneging of contracts, it's a wonder I looked this good!
	(A beat.)
CAROL	I want to live life again, though, Rob.
	(A beat.)
ROB	I know you do!
	(A beat.)
CAROL	I mean, I didn't want you to go, you know!
	(A beat.)
ROB	Why, did you think that I did? Because you're bloody wrong, there!
CAROL	Of course not!
	(A beat.)
ROB	I mean, not seeing Adam grow up and graduate, not seeing Carrie meet someone and settle down. Did you think I wanted a brain tumour? *(A beat.)* I wouldn't wish it on my worst enemy, to be honest. *(A beat.)* And I know that they did everything in the NHS; talk about a system under stress. Bless 'em! *(A beat.)* I didn't want

to go, in fact. I don't know anybody who does!
The only good thing about it is that you don't
have to deal with the VAT man. Everything else
about dying is absolute shite, mate, let me tell
you! (*A beat.*) And I don't know whether it's too
early or not; who's to say? (*A beat.*) But I know
this much. (*A beat.*) I miss you. I really miss you!

(ROB *pecks* CAROL *kindly on the cheek and then
slowly moves to exit upstage.* CAROL *watches
him go and is very upset.*)

CAROL

Rob, Rob! Rob? (*A beat.*) I wish he'd just say
what he means! I wish he would just actually
say what he means for once; be straightforward.
(*A beat.*) But he never was; he was so good with
words that you sometimes had no idea what
he was on about. I mean, what was I supposed
to do? Just muddle through, making a mess of
almost everything I touch? Because you're never
certain, are you? (*A beat.*) You know; in life,
we're really never certain.

[LXQ] [SQ]

(CAROL *drifts to an upstage resting position
behind the counter where she is able to have
a little sip of a coffee. Meanwhile,* DON *enters.
He has mud on his face, mounts a bike and
starts working hard. He is caught in a spotlight
downstage. It is evening. A light on his bike
helmet shines against the dark.*)

DON

Every night I try to forget the day; the old
women with pale faces and sallow cheeks, with
sunken eyes, like the blood's been drained,
the walking sacks of humanity dropped at
Outpatients. (DON *adjusts his position, and is
angry.*) If I could wave a magic wand, I would.
If I could cure the lot of 'em, I would! (*A beat.*)
I see mi Mam in them, lost, a number, caught

in the system; I see Jean in them. Hobbling in with their swollen feet and puffy faces, smelling of chip fat and nylon sheets. (*A beat.*) I see a nation teetering on the edge of loneliness, in fear of high food prices and endless credit. (*He readjusts his position.*) I see shops shutting, people on the street, vaping and smoking and stuffing thessens wi'burgers, coz they can't afford owt else. (*A beat.*) I see a bloated mass we now call the English! (*He repositions himself.*) And I can't stand still. Can't relax, sit down, stay quiet. Can't sleep! I can't turn a blind eye. (*A beat.*) I want to help, but what can I do? All I know is that something doesn't fit; something doesn't ring true. (*He pedals more. He begins to slow down and sits up on the bike. He is breathless; this has been cathartic.*) And I texted Carol to say that I'd find the money, that I wanted to go! I did extra shifts, saved up, sold stuff, went without food for two weeks, lived on bread and water like a prisoner in solitary, because that's what it's been like, if you wanna know t' truth! (*A beat.*) And I felt completely guilty, like I was betraying everything Jean and I stood for . . . (*A beat.*) I mean, what the hell would she have said?

(JEAN *enters; she is younger and well, and as feisty as we saw her during the miners' strike. She is aggressive and smokes.* DON *is embarrassed by his behaviour in front of his dead wife.*)

JEAN   'You playing at?

DON   Oh, don't!

JEAN   You don't even know her.

DON   I know that, don't I? Don't tell me what I already know!

JEAN	And you're going where?
DON	Florence!
JEAN	Bloody Florence?
DON	Listen, honestly . . .
JEAN	Bloody Florence?
DON	She says it's nice . . .
JEAN	Bloody Florence, now?
DON	It's the seat of the Renaissance, she says.
JEAN	Oh, the bloody Renaissance?
JEAN	Do you fancy her?
DON	Eh?
JEAN	Do you?
DON	Wow!
JEAN	You do!
DON	Jean, I'm nearly sixty-five.
JEAN	Lucky you!
DON	Hey, listen!
JEAN	I wish I was nearly sixty-five.
DON	Hey, I'm lucky; I can still put my own socks on. Don't make this any more difficult than it should be.
JEAN	Stay with your own creed, you said. That's what the strike was about, you said. Stand together, you said. Now look at you!

DON	What?
JEAN	Bloody Florence, now!
DON	Eh?
JEAN	A bloody class traitor, that's what you are.
DON	How am I?
JEAN	You've changed, you have!
DON	How have I?
JEAN	You've bloody changed!

[LXQ]

(JEAN *has evaporated upstage and* DON *is back-pedalling hard, talking to himself.*)

DON   I'm on my bloody own here, you do know that, don't you? Our Wayne's back in Armley after that Post Office job in Wetherby, and I never hear a frigging word from our Jeff. I'm frightened of spiralling downwards, cock; can you not see that? (*A beat.*) Well what the hell am I supposed to do? I've got nowhere to go, and no one to talk to. What did you want me to do; become a frigging monk? Jean? Jean! Jean!

[LXQ] [SQ]

(*Music swells.* DON *exits from the bike upstage as the lights fade and* CAROL *is stood downstage, with the sweeping brush very much as we saw her at the beginning the play. Speaks to the audience.*)

CAROL   And he was right about the cost, because when we came to work it out, with the bike hire and the hotels and villas and the trains, it was nearer to three-and-a-half grand, but it was too late by then; we'd both said we'd do it! But, I did come up with a money-saving idea, which made us both laugh!

[LXQ] [SQ]

(DON *enters upstage, and now has a more advanced cycling top, and carries a helmet. He stands upstage near the tandem as the lights change. Don is inspecting the tandem.*)

DON	Give over!
CAROL	What do you think?
DON	Really?
CAROL	Yes!

(CAROL *moves upstage to* DON *and the tandem.*)

DON	Will it get us there?
CAROL	It better do; I've just bought it!
DON	Well who'll be steering?
CAROL	That'll be me.
DON	Well that'll be a laugh, then!
CAROL	Why will it?
DON	Because I've seen your driving!
CAROL	What do you mean by that?

(*A beat.*)

DON	So I'm in the boiler house?
CAROL	It's called the stoker!

DON   Exactly!

             (*A beat.*)

CAROL   It's seventy miles to Hull, the first day.

DON   Well that's nowt; what about the luggage?

CAROL   They pick it up, and it'll be at the hotels by the
             time we arrive each night.

DON   And are we going to practise on this?

CAROL   That's why I bought it; we can leave it in here at
             night.

DON   That's if the kids don't break in and steal it!

CAROL   They reckon if we do two hundred miles a week
             for the next four weeks, we should stand a
             chance.

DON   A chance of what?

CAROL   Of still being able to walk when we come back!

             (*A beat.*)

DON   Well I hope nobody sees me on that.

CAROL   Yes, I know what you mean!

DON   What are we doing?

CAROL   I know, it's madness!

DON   When are we looking to go?

CAROL   June 23rd.

DON   Oh right, good timing.

CAROL	And that was it! We started training on the tandem.
DON	And what a joke that was!
CAROL	Honestly, funny!
DON	It was like a bloody *Carry On* film!

(*Both speak to the audience.*)

CAROL	I'd arranged cover at the café, and before we knew it I was about to set off on a bike ride with a man I had known for less than five months.
DON	After four weeks' training she could hardly walk, she couldn't bear to sit down, and she'd developed tennis elbow (don't ask me how), and we only had a thousand miles ahead of us!
CAROL	But one thing was for sure, it was going to be anything but dull!
DON	June 23rd, 2016, we set off from York at half-two, to get the ferry that night.
CAROL	And after a break in Beverley, to look in the Minster and have a coffee at the Café Velo, we were all set for the final ride into Hull.

(DON *and* CAROL *action to put on their helmets.*)

[LXQ] [SQ]

(DON *and* CAROL *prepare to mount the tandem, almost ritualistically. They don cycling windjammers and put on their helmets. It is a late 23rd June evening in 2016. They are lit in a pool of light which gives us a sense of movement, and although they are pedalling in unison, when they speak to each other they have to shout to the point of it being almost impossible.*)

CAROL	You still there?
DON	What?
CAROL	You still there?
DON	Just about!
CAROL	Only six hundred yards to the ferry port.
DON	Just keep going!
CAROL	If I go the wrong way now, just prod me.
DON	If you go wrong now, I'll strangle you!
CAROL	What?
DON	Are you actually pedalling?
CAROL	What?
DON	My thighs are bursting!
CAROL	What?
DON	Just keep going!
CAROL	What?

(DON *calls out.*)

DON	Lorry!
CAROL	Lorry!

(*They wobble a lorry passes them.*)

DON	Bloody idiot!
CAROL	Bloody idiot!

DON	Car!
CAROL	Car!
DON	Arsehole!

(*They pedal for a while.*)

CAROL	Did you vote then, Don?
DON	What?
CAROL	Did you vote?
DON	This morning.
CAROL	In or out?
DON	Me! I voted out.
CAROL	You haven't got a chance.
DON	Shame!
CAROL	It'll be a bit weird hearing the result and us being in Europe.
DON	Well, the people have spoken.
CAROL	They reckon there's been a big turnout, don't they?

(*A beat.*)

DON	Lorry!
CAROL	Lorry!

(*They wobble as a lorry passes.*)

DON	Bloody idiot!
CAROL	Arsehole!

DON	What?
CAROL	Arsehole!
DON	Me?
CAROL	The Lorry!
DON	Car!
CAROL	Car!
DON	Arsehole.
CAROL	Bloody idiot!

(*They wobble once more.*)

DON	We should have got a phone each.
CAROL	Why's that?
DON	Because I haven't really heard a word you've been saying for the last three hours!
CAROL	What?

(*They wobble as traffic passes them.*)

DON	Dumper truck!
CAROL	Dumper truck!
DON	Coach!
CAROL	Coach!
DON	Bloody idiots!
CAROL	Oh, my knees!

(CAROL *sits high in the seat.* DON *is still pedalling.*)

DON	Argh!
CAROL	Oh!
DON	Argh!!

(*A beat.*)

CAROL	How do you feel?

(*A beat.*)

DON	Well I stink of sweat, and my keks are stuck to me.

(*A beat.*)

CAROL	That's good to know, then!

[LXQ] [SQ]

(DON *and* CAROL *dismount the bike and both demonstrate in a highly comical way that they can hardly walk. With their cycling gear they certainly don't look fit for European travel. As they walk downstage they collect a backpack each and the lights change to a pool of light.*)

DON	Ooh!
CAROL	I don't know where I ache the most.
DON	I do!
CAROL	Don't tell me!

(*A beat.*)

DON	Don't worry, I won't!

(*A beat.*)

CAROL	Well that's the first fifty miles done.

DON	Yes, we're just warming up, aren't we?
	(A beat.)
CAROL	Well I'm frying in this, so you could say that.
DON	Well done, mate!
	(CAROL *speaks to the audience.*)
CAROL	I had a broken toe, my ankles were bleeding and my face was so chapped from the sun and the wind that I looked like a chipmunk! *(A beat.)* I got on the boat, climbed into the bunk and fell asleep.
DON	I was so tired that I slept on the toilet! And I'll tell you this; the next morning, as we headed for breakfast, people looked at us differently!
CAROL	Yes, there was certainly something in the air! And then we suddenly realised what it was. *(A beat.)* That night, the UK had voted, by fifty-one point nine percent to forty-eight point one percent, to leave the European Union.
DON	And there we were!
CAROL	Just about to start our European adventure . . .
DON	You couldn't've bloody made it up, could you?
CAROL	And as we headed back to the tandem, one thing was for sure . . .
DON	Yes, there was no turning back now!
	(The music swells and the lights fade as they begin to pedal on the tandem once more.)
	(End of Act One.)

ACT TWO

House lights fade. [SQ]

DON and CAROL are on a busy slip road of a dual carriageway. As large trucks pass them, the tandem wobbles. The screen plays images of cycling to counterpoint their lack of actual movement, but they pedal easily, as there is no chain on the bike. The work is hard and they speak loudly and heavily.

DON   Alright?

CAROL   Yes!

               (*A beat.*)

DON   Lorry!

CAROL   Lorry!

               (DON *looks behind.*)

DON   Car!

CAROL   Car!

               (DON *looks behind.*)

DON   Boat!

CAROL   Boat?

DON   On a lorry!

               (*They pedal on.*)

CAROL   We should hit a cycle route up here on the left.

               (DON *looks behind.*)

DON   Lorry!

CAROL   Lorry!

               (*They wobble.*)

DON   Bloody hell, that wa' close!

               (*A beat.*)

CAROL   I can't believe we're out of Europe.

DON   We will be out of Europe if one of these lorries
               hits us!

CAROL   Adam was having a fit when I spoke to him
               this morning. Been up all night. He said the
               country was in shock. Said there was a girl from
               Cambridge University been on breakfast telly
               crying because she'd thought the country had
               let her down. I just can't believe that we voted
               out.

DON   No, you said!

CAROL   London voted remain! Well I expected that. All
               the big cities voted that way. It's like we're all
               rednecks up north, isn't it? I don't know what
               they'll think we are.

DON   I've not looked at it, so I can't really say. (DON
               looks behind.) Look out, I don't know what this
               is. Half a house, I think!

CAROL   That might be somebody moving out already.

               (*They wobble on the bike.* DON *looks behind
               him.*)

DON   Lorry!

CAROL   Lorry!

               (DON *looks.*)

DON	Lorry!
CAROL	Lorry!
	(DON *looks*.)
DON	Lorry!
CAROL	Lorry!
DON	A lot of lorries!
CAROL	There'll be massive trade tariffs, won't there? I wouldn't fancy going all the way to China to do trade.
DON	Not on a bike!
CAROL	There's all the border controls, free movement of people.
	(DON *looks behind them*.)
DON	Lorry!
	(*They wobble even more*.)
BOTH	Wow!
DON	Bloody idiot!
CAROL	I think he was English.
DON	Arsehole!
	(*They pedal on*.)
CAROL	I don't think he could hear you.
DON	It's too busy . . . let's push it!
CAROL	I can't push it too much.

DON	Why not?
CAROL	Because my lunch is in my mouth!
DON	Come on, Carol, keep it going!
	(They pedal on as the lights fade and the music plays.)
	[LXQ] [SQ]
	(Much later. DON looks around him. They are clearly in a quiet part of Belgium. As it is quieter, they don't need to shout so loudly when they speak to each other.)
CAROL	Smoother, now!
	(A beat.)
DON	Are you sure this is right, though?
CAROL	Hope so. My phone's about to die, so . . .
DON	Hey?
CAROL	I said, my sat nav's on the blink.
DON	That's good, then!
CAROL	It says turn left.
DON	There are no lefts!
CAROL	We've already turned left.
DON	Was it the right left?
CAROL	I've no idea; it could have been the wrong left!
DON	Right!
CAROL	No, left!

DON   Oh, don't. We sound like the Chuckle Brothers!

CAROL   Give it another quarter of an hour and see what
             comes up.

DON   It might be that spag bol!

CAROL   Yes, it might be!

             (*They pedal on.*)

             [LXQ] [SQ]

             (*Much later. As the lights come back up we now
             get a sense that the tandem is in the middle of
             nowhere on a cycle track by a canal bank. DON
             has a medium-size map which he is getting out
             of the front pocket on his top, and is sat astride
             the tandem. CAROL has dismounted and they
             have lost some of their enthusiasm for the route.
             The film on the screen reflects their current
             situation.*)

DON   Well, it's not on here!

CAROL   Have you got the right map?

DON   Well, I've only got this one, so . . .

             (*A beat.*)

CAROL   Because if we get behind with the connections
             we're in a mess! The train tickets are non-
             transferable.

DON   Oh, that's good!

             (*A beat.*)

CAROL   And I don't know about you, but I feel
             exhausted! I don't think I'll be able to pedal all
             the way back to the motorway.

(*A beat.*)

DON	We should've turned back sooner!
CAROL	Well I suppose we had no idea.
DON	No idea about what?
CAROL	That we were lost!

(*A beat.*)

DON	Well it's doesn't look so good, does it?
CAROL	We're in the middle of nowhere, aren't we?
DON	Yes, we're in the middle of nowhere!

(*There is a moment and they become more relaxed, though it is clear that* CAROL *is anxious.*)

CAROL	Oh hell! Well, this is a dog's breakfast!
DON	A dog's what?
CAROL	It'll be dark in an hour. (*A beat.*) Why has it taken us so long?
DON	What, to discover we're lost, or to get lost?

(*A beat.*)

CAROL	So, what do you reckon?

(*A beat.*)

DON	Well, we've got three options haven't we? We go back . . .
CAROL	Go back?
DON	Yes.

CAROL   What, all that way?

               (*A beat.*)

DON   Or we go on.

CAROL   Yes, but where to? . . .

DON   To wherever we were supposed to be going.

CAROL   Or?

               (*A beat.*)

DON   Or, we stop here.

CAROL   What?

               (*A beat.*)

DON   Well, we're not going to get to Ghent tonight,
               are we, and we're not going to get to the
               Oudenaarde Cycling Museum, or whatever it's
               called, because we're miles out on the map.

               (*A beat.*)

CAROL   Can't we go back?

DON   Well, I'm happy to go back, but I thought you
               were too tired.

CAROL   Well I am, but . . .

DON   I mean, I don't fancy that main road in the
               bloody dark, but . . .

               (*A beat.*)

CAROL   Well I don't know what to suggest, to be
               honest.

               (*A beat.*)

DON	Well, I say we stay here!
CAROL	In the middle of a field?
	(*A beat.*)
DON	Well we haven't got many options left, have we?
	(*A beat.*)
CAROL	And what are we going to do, sleep under the stars?
DON	Well I'm for pushing on, but if you're knackered . . .
	(*A beat.*)
CAROL	Well I don't want to overdo it; we've got a thousand miles to go, haven't we?
DON	We have indeed.
	(*A beat.*)
CAROL	So are we stopping here, then?
	(*A beat.*)
DON	Listen, there was a little garage sort of thing about half a mile back. I'll go and see if they've got any blankets or sommat.
CAROL	What?
	(*A beat.*)
DON	I'll go back and see if they can help.
CAROL	And what shall I do?
DON	You wait here.

(*A beat.*)

CAROL   With the bike?

DON   Well I can hardly ride the bike on my own, can
          I? I'll jog!

(*A beat.*)

CAROL   And how long will that take?

DON   I dunno; forty minutes, maybe shorter. I'll just
          see what they've got.

(*A beat.*)

CAROL   What, me just stay with the bike till it gets dark?

DON   Yes, just sit in the hedge bottom.

CAROL   Eh?

DON   Well you're out of the wind, then, aren't you.

(*A beat.*)

CAROL   And how are we going to sleep in the hedge
          bottom?

DON   Well we probably won't get any sleep, but I
          can't see an alternative, can you? (*A beat.*) Let
          me go and see what I can do.

(*A beat.*)

CAROL   Well I don't know if I fancy that, Don, to be
          honest!

(*A beat.*)

DON   Well we haven't got much choice, have we?
          And if your phone's dead we can't call anybody.

CAROL   Well where's your phone?

DON   In a drawer at home in the kitchen!

               (*A beat.*)

CAROL   Can't believe this! Stuck in the middle of
               nowhere with a bloody Brexiteer.

DON   Oh, funny!

CAROL   Well how do I know that'll you'll come back
               for me, Don? "Out means out," doesn't it,
               according to your leader!

DON   Hey, well it was all about Brexit this morning,
               wasn't it?

CAROL   Bloody Brexit!

DON   If you'd've come off the phone, your battery
               wouldn't have died and we wouldn't be lost!

CAROL   I was actually speaking with my son!

DON   Lucky you!

CAROL   What?

DON   Oh, just relax!

CAROL   Relax? We're in the middle of bloody nowhere!

DON   Well what else can we do?

CAROL   It's just that I get anxious on my own.

DON   Eh?

CAROL   I get anxious when I'm left on my own.

DON   Well you're not on your own, are you? There's
               some cows over there! (DON *takes a Mars*

Protein bar from his windjammer pocket.) Here, have a Mars bar and save the wrapper and cover yourself in it!

CAROL   Cheers, mate!

DON   I'll be back with sommat, don't you worry about that. Nobody dies on my watch!

CAROL   Oh, cheers for that!

DON   Well what did you want me to say? We're both gunna perish and be eaten by a wolf!

CAROL   And do you think that that's not going to make me more anxious?

             [LXQ] [SQ]

             (DON *exits the tandem area and collects a small pop-up tent, which he erects in the next scene-change state.*)

DON   So I jogs back about half a mile to this garage thing, rate, and she wa' rate, coz the light drops very quick over there. Anyway, as it turns out, I dropped three bells, but it didn't seem to cheer her up!

             (*The LX signifies it is darker at night and* DON *unsheaths the pop-up tent and lets it pop up.* DON *and* CAROL *survey the scene.*)

CAROL   Oh, right!

DON   What's up with this?

CAROL   That's the big idea, is it?

DON   Please yourself, like . . .

(*By using LED torches,* CAROL *and* DON *make their way into the small tent. It is cosy, to say the least. The audience only hear what is going on inside the tent, and the only thing they can see is illuminated by the small helmet-lights and the LED lights.* CAROL *and* DON *have taken their helmets off, and their sunglasses.*)

CAROL   Do you think you can sleep in that?

DON   We'll soon find out.

CAROL   Well at least it's not cold.

DON   Cold? I'm melting in this lycra.

               (*They begin to tackle the tent.*)

CAROL   I didn't know you could speak any Flemish, Don. Mind you, they all speak English, don't they . . . waste of time now, but . . .

DON   I didn't need to speak any Flemish, did I?

CAROL   Why, how much was it?

DON   No idea, I just took it!

CAROL   Eh?

DON   It was in a trailer around the back.

               (*A beat.*)

CAROL   I'm on holiday with a bloody felon, now!

DON   Don't worry about it!

               (*They crawl inside the tent.*)

CAROL   Cosy, anyway!

DON	That's an understatement, isn't it? (*A beat.*) You still feel anxious?
CAROL	Well, I feel a bit claustrophobic, to be honest!
DON	It's rate! (*A beat.*) If I could just move my leg from under me!
CAROL	This is good; I'm actually sleeping with the enemy, now!
DON	Yes, I could say the same.
CAROL	I just hope we don't miss the train.
DON	Well there's nowt to be anxious about in here, is there?
CAROL	Unless we run out of oxygen.
DON	Last night I slept on t' loo; tonight I feel like Harry Houdini!
CAROL	Well, things can only get better.
DON	Oh, don't start with that, for God's sake!

(*Silence.*)

CAROL	What's that dripping sound, Don?
DON	That's the beads of sweat dripping from me head coz I'm absolutely bloody roasting!

[LXQ] [SQ]

(*Lights fade, and as they touch black they come back up suggesting a very early misty morning. We can hear birdsong as the zip of the tent is unzipped and* DON *less-than-elegantly emerges from the tent, followed closely by* CAROL. *Both are stiff, and moan commensurately.*)

Carol	Urgh!
	(*A beat.*)
Don	You sleep?
Carol	No!
Don	Neither did I; the cow bells kept me awake!
	(*They stretch to their feet.*)
Carol	How are we for time?
	(Don *glances at his watch.* Carol *and* Don *get to their feet through the last dialogue; they now have to address the tent. The sheath it came in is close by.*)
Don	Let's get this down.
Carol	Do you know how to do it?
	(*A beat.*)
Don	Well it went up easily enough.
Carol	That's good, then!
	(*A beat.*)
Don	Let's have a look.
Carol	Are you going to take it back?
Don	Am I hell!
Carol	Why not?
Don	Well, what if we get lost again? (Don *starts to fold down the two-second tent, which proves to be harder than he imagined possible.*) Yellow to yellow. That's that! Then fold it under. (Don

attempts to fold the tent.) Red to red. (DON
*attempts to follow the tent further, but it beats
him.*) Hang on, what is it? Blue to blue? (DON
*attempts another go at folding the tent but it
defeats him.*) It's one of them that takes two
seconds to put up.

(*A beat.*)

CAROL   Yes, and a year to put down!

DON   I will put it down in a minute; I'll rip the
               sodding thing to bits!

               (*A beat.*)

CAROL   Can I help?

DON   No, it's rate!

               (DON *stands and looks at the tent for a moment,
               and then attacks it with vigour and folds it
               precisely in the sheath in a neat movement.
               Then he puts the folded and sheathed tent on
               his back. They put their helmets back on and
               head towards the tandem area.*)

               Right, that's it; back on the bike!

               (DON *still has the tent attached to his back and
               they both wear helmets and sunglasses, which
               they remove as they set up the next location.
               CAROL puts a red-and-white tablecloth on the
               keel table. She gets bottle of wine and a glass
               from behind the counter, and DON sits with a
               bottle of water.*)

CAROL   Oh yes, absolutely true! We got to Ghent just
               in time for the train to Brussels, and then on to
               Paris.

DON   What a run that wa'!

CAROL	And we never mentioned Brexit again.
DON	In fact we didn't talk about it all the way down through France and into Geneva!
CAROL	Yes, it was the elephant on the bike.
DON	Funny!
CAROL	Four days later when we finally arrived in Pisa on the train, we'd hardly spoken at all, to be honest, and this was supposed to be the start of a relaxing cycling holiday through the Italian countryside!
DON	We stayed in this little, what was it called? . . .
CAROL	An agriturismo!
DON	Basically a cycling café with an orchard, on the edge of Pisa, run by a bloke who had been involved with the Tour de Italy.
CAROL	Years ago.
DON	Yes, he must have weighed thirty stone!
CAROL	And it was warm, wasn't it?
DON	There was like a outside area overlooking the countryside, and what a view that wa'!
	[LXQ] [SQ]
	(*Italian accordion music. The LX suggest a balmy evening.*)
DON	This is alrate, isn't it?
	(CAROL *sips her wine.*)
CAROL	Sure you don't want a glass of wine or a beer or something?

(*A beat.*)

DON   Gave that up years ago.

CAROL   Really?

DON   Oh aye.

(*A beat.*)

CAROL   You can just have one, can't you?

DON   No!

CAROL   Oh, right.

(*A beat.*)

DON   I can't just have one.

CAROL   Why not?

DON   Because then I want another one. Then another one. Then another one!

CAROL   Oh dear!

DON   No, I've had my share, to be honest. (*A beat.*) In fact, to be rate, I think that I've had somebody else's share and all!

CAROL   Like that, was it?

DON   Well it's a drug, isn't it?

(*A beat.*)

CAROL   Spoke to Adam; he's still on fire. He reckons they should have another vote.

DON   Another one?

CAROL   That's what they're saying.

DON	Took us a million years to have one referendum. I can't see 'em having another one straight away.

(*A beat.*)

CAROL	I don't know; you get into a bubble and you think everyone thinks like you do. (*A beat.*) I mean, I voted remain and you think everybody else you know did!

(*A beat.*)

DON	Well it was close, Carol.
CAROL	I suppose so.
DON	Could've gone either way!

(*A beat.*)

CAROL	The thing is, if you're not careful, you forget what real life's all about. That's what Rob used to say.

(*A beat.*)

DON	Well I don't, I can tell you that.
CAROL	No, but you know what I mean? (*A beat.*) I'm just saying that you think everybody's on the same page as you are. (*A beat.*) Yorkshire voted mostly for Brexit, so you'll be pleased to hear that! York and Leeds voted remain. Hull, Wakefield and Sheffield, all massive out votes, according to Adam. (*A beat.*) And he's going anyway, David Cameron.
DON	Is he?
CAROL	Adam said! So they're going to have to find somebody else to sort it out. Thrown his teddy

out the cot! (*A beat.*) I'm really fearful for the
future, to be honest.

(*A beat.*)

Don   What have we got tomorrow?

Carol   Only thirty miles.

(*A beat.*)

Don   Nowt, that! That run down to Geneva's a killer,
           though. Mind you, Eddy Merckx did that on one
           of the Tour de France runs, and they reckon he
           was having a heart attack.

Carol   Really?

Don   What a bloody animal!

Carol   Well I don't suppose they called him "The
           Cannibal" for nothing.

Don   No, I don't suppose.

(*A beat.*)

Carol   I think it was a bit too much for me, to be
           honest. I was pleased to get on the train.

Don   Nice trains!

Carol   Not like ours.

Don   Bang on time.

Carol   If we had trains like that . . .

Don   Be fewer lorries on the road; mind you, there's
           tons over here, so how does that work? (*A beat.*)
           More space, though!

(*A beat.*)

CAROL	You should see first class!
	(*A beat.*)
DON	I've never been first class, ever!
	(*A beat.*)
CAROL	Listen, I er . . . I suppose if we're going to enjoy this, Don, we'll have to agree to disagree, you know, about Brexit. I mean there's no need to let it spoil Italy, is there?
DON	Suits me!
CAROL	There's some great things to see; we can see the Leaning Tower tomorrow, and then we're down to Lucca, Puccini's birthplace. Then Vinci. Leonardo's birthplace, and when we get to Florence . . .
DON	Florence Nightingale's birthplace!
CAROL	Eh?
DON	I'm joking!
	(*A beat.*)
CAROL	No, there's the Uffizi Gallery, Michelangelo's David; it's pretty stunning! There's no need for us to be Cameron and Corbyn, so . . .
	(*A beat.*)
DON	Well they're all the same to me . . .
CAROL	Well I think that those two are about as different as you could get, but . . .
DON	Well they're all clowns, so . . .
CAROL	How come?

DON   Well it's a circus, isn't it? And you allus get
               clowns in a circus!

               (*A beat.*)

CAROL   So what was it for you, then? All about
               immigration?

DON   What?

CAROL   That's what they reckon?

DON   What you saying; that I'm a racist?

CAROL   Well . . .

DON   What would you do if I said I was?

CAROL   What could I do?

               (*A beat.*)

DON   Do you think that everybody who voted out are
               racists?

CAROL   Quite possibly.

DON   What?

CAROL   There is a kind of implicit suggestion; you can
               see that, surely?

DON   I'm not a racist, Carol!

CAROL   Well that's a relief! I thought for a moment I
               was stuck on a tandem with a member of the
               Ku Klux Klan!

DON   I'm not a racist, I'm not homophobic, I'm not
               religious. I worked wi' Polish lads in t' pits, I
               worked with Syrians on security and I work with
               every nation in NHS!

CAROL   Exactly!

DON   Half the consultants are immigrants, you know
             that, don't you? Him what did my Mam's heart
             was Turkish! I put some fencing in for him. (A
             beat.) Blunket let too many in, that's a raw fact.
             Sixty thousand, they said, and how many came
             in?

CAROL   Six hundred thousand!

DON   Yes, on his watch, which was a bit awkward!
             (A beat.) No, I might look and sound like a
             redneck, Carol, but . . . they assumed we were
             going to remain; they were arrogant enough
             to think we'd vote the way they wanted us to.
             (A beat.) Well I was fed up o' being used to be
             rate; that's why I voted out.

CAROL   Used?

DON   As a threat. Patronised by an elite that don't
             want to know us most of the time! Who don't
             listen to us most of the time. Look at the Iraq
             war, when nearly a million marched on London;
             what did they do, listen to them? Look at t'
             strike, all that evidence about coal. Look at
             China opening a pit every drop of a hat; did
             they listen to us then?

CAROL   Well that's fair.

DON   During t' strike they tried to put us down, wipe
             us out, and they made a pretty good job, and
             now they're asking us what we wanted! What
             did they think it was, Christmas? (A beat.) I'll tell
             you what I want! I want uz jobs back, I want
             uz communities back! (A beat.) For clever men,
             they've got short memories! Too much port,
             maybe!

             (A beat.)

CAROL	So it was about revenge?
DON	Personally, for me, a little bit. And respect!
	(*A beat.*)
CAROL	Respect?
DON	I don't respect them, because they don't respect me! They don't respect me, and they don't respect the people I work with; how can they? They have no empathy, they don't understand us! They don't shop where I shop, travel on same buses, live where I live, talk wi't' same people as I talk to, have t' same income, go on't' same holidays . . .
CAROL	Well we can't all be the same, Don.
DON	Tha' can't watch 'em fending and proving on't' telly and respect 'em, can you?
CAROL	Well . . .
DON	I lost respect for t' MP's when they stopped being connected to t' unions!
CAROL	Well that was seriously flawed!
DON	Well at least they knew what it wa' like to be a working man. This lot are all about thessens!
CAROL	Not all of them!
DON	Give up!
CAROL	And that's not much of a generalisation, is it, Don? Come on, give them a chance!
DON	Thee tell me, how many have had proper jobs? No, no, I tell thee what, thee tell me how many haven't been to university. In fact I bet they all

went to same bloody university knowing how
it all works! (*A beat.*) Come on, Carol, I wasn't
born yesterday. Give me a bit of bloody credit.
I'm nearly sixty-two; I've buried my wife and
my Mam and Dad. Does tha' think I don't know
how many beans mek five?

CAROL   So they're all tarred with the same brush; do
you honestly believe that of all of them?

DON   If only one had been caught with their pants
down, or their hand in t' till, or cheating, or
lying, or bending bloody rules, I'd say fair! But
it isn't just one, is it?

CAROL   Well, no . . . sadly.

DON   And them that haven't been doing that must be
thinking: what a set of arseholes am I working
wi' here? (*A beat.*) And when they've done wi'
Westminster, they're on't' telly, or 'radio, or on
train journeys, or *Dancing on Ice*, or they're
bringing a book out! (*A beat.*) I'm telling thee,
it's nowt but a finishing school for *Celebrity Big
Brother!*

(CAROL *laughs easily.*)

CAROL   Well there is some truth in that.

DON   Bloody gravy train!

CAROL   Possibly!

DON   Giving thessen's pay rises when they feel like it!

CAROL   Well . . .

DON   What was it, nine percent? And public service
wages were on standstill; and we look at 'em
and think, what planet are they on? We're stood
there holding our nuts while they do what the

sodding hell they like. "Tell thee what, Cecil,
I vote we have a pay rise, what do you vote? I
vote t' same as thee, Cedric! Motion passed."

CAROL   That's funny!

DON   Funny is what is isn't! Then they're not
               disclosing this, that and t' bloody other! "Oh,
               I forgot about my third house. Oh, I forgot my
               kids were working for me. Oh, I forgot that an
               Italian billionaire had just paid off my mortgage;
               slipped my mind, that!"

CAROL   You should be on the telly, Don!

DON   Well I'd be better than them!

CAROL   You would!

DON   Did they think we'd not spotted all that? (*A
               beat.*) But the main reason, rate, if you want
               to know . . . the main reason I voted out, was
               because of the money!

CAROL   What money?

DON   The three hundred and fifty million a week
               they've promised t' NHS!

CAROL   Do you actually think that they're going to do
               that?

DON   Why wouldn't they?

CAROL   Seriously?

DON   Yes!

CAROL   Honestly?

DON   Get the money out!

CAROL   Honestly?

DON   I'm being serious; get that money out and stick
               it in NHS. It's on its chuffin' knees! Eighteen
               billion that'd be, a year! Get it back, get it paid,
               let's get some of these folks sorted. There's old
               women dying in corridors; I mean we're not a
               third-world country, are we?

CAROL   They're not going to do that, though.

DON   They'd better!

CAROL   They're not!

DON   Why not?

CAROL   Because they're playing with you!

               (*A beat.*)

DON   How are they?

CAROL   Give it three months and that big red bus will
               have had a respray, and they idea will be dead!
               Because they didn't expect to win; they didn't
               expect to have to come out, either.

DON   Well if these are men of integrity and
               substance.

CAROL   Which they're not, according to you! You've
               said they're not; you don't trust 'em as far
               as you could throw them, but you believed
               them on the NHS. How perverse is that? Talk
               about double Dutch. Come on, Don, listen to
               yourself! I hate them, but I'll vote for them;
               what?

DON   I voted for that money, that's what I voted for!

CAROL   It was absolute hogwash, though!

DON   They're gunna do that and I'll tell thee why:
               because nobody can be that deceiving and get
               away wi' it! You mark my words, when all this
               has died down, that money'll be going to t' NHS.

CAROL   No!

DON   I'm telling you, Carol, it's nailed on!

CAROL   Fifty quid!

DON   Fifty quid?

CAROL   Fifty quid that you're wrong.

DON   I'll have bloody five hundred quid on that! They
               can't do it, otherwise, can't you see that? It's
               too big a bluff for it not to be rate!

CAROL   Fifty quid?

DON   Alrate, fifty quid!

               (CAROL and DON shake on their large bet.)

CAROL   I can't wait for that!

DON   Because, you see, if that was a lie, then
               whoever wa' involved wi' it would be dead in
               the water. Their careers would be over, they'll
               disappear from public life and never get another
               job.

CAROL   It's water off a duck's back, Don.

DON   Fifty quid, mate!

               (CAROL shouts aggressively; it makes her dizzy.)

CAROL   They don't give a toss what you think! They
               just wanted you to vote for them for their own

benefit! (CAROL *swoons slightly.*) Oh hell! Just gone bloody dizzy!

(DON *notices.*)

DON   Hey, are you alrate?

               (*A beat.*)

CAROL   I don't know, to be honest.

DON   Coz you look bloody awful!

               (*A beat.*)

CAROL   Is it warm?

DON   Yes, it's roasting!

               (*A beat.*)

CAROL   Ohh!

DON   What?

               (*A beat.*)

CAROL   I've just gone feeling like shit.

DON   You look it!

               (CAROL *convulses.*)

CAROL   I feel really light-headed!

DON   Well, it is boiling.

               (CAROL *feels her upper chest.*)

CAROL   I feel really tight, right across here! Right tight across my chest . . . and my arm.

               (*A beat.*)

DON   Oh bloody hell, that's not good.

CAROL   Oh I feel bloody . . .

DON   Right!

CAROL   What?

DON   Hospital!

CAROL   What?

DON   Yes!

CAROL   Oh no!

             (DON *feels her head*.)

DON   You're too warm for my liking.

CAROL   I'm not going to hospital!

DON   You are!

CAROL   I'm not!

DON   Yes you are!

CAROL   No, I'm not!

DON   Yes you bloody are!

CAROL   No, I'm bloody not!

DON   Hey, listen . . . !

CAROL   You listen, you silly oaf; I'm going to no
             hospital. You're a porter at Pontefract, not Dr
             Christian Barnard. Get the message; I'm going
             to no bloody hospital in the middle of the night!

             [LXQ] [SQ]

(*As the lights come up on the tandem* DON
is pedalling from the front seat and CAROL *is
perched on the saddle at the back of the bike,
sat sideways.*)

DON   Chest pains, you're sweating, and you're a
           woman of a certain age. We've got to check it
           out!

CAROL   This is bloody crackers!

DON   Safety first, mate.

CAROL   Why couldn't the landlord take us?

DON   Did you see him? He couldn't stand up, for a
           start!

CAROL   I thought you might have stolen his car!

DON   Funny.

CAROL   It's not like the NHS, you know; there'll be a
           charge.

DON   Cross that bridge when we come to it.

CAROL   I think it's probably just indigestion!

DON   Just sit back and enjoy the ride.

CAROL   How do you know where the hospital is?

DON   I always find out where the hospitals are! (*A
           beat.*) Jean was ill for so long, I got into the
           habit.

CAROL   That's great, but a bit sad, Don.

DON   Yes, I know. Jean always said that I was a
           prophet of doom.

CAROL   Oh, bloody wonderful! (CAROL *looks behind her.*) Look out, scooter!

DON   Scooter!

BOTH   Bloody idiot!

             [LXQ] [SQ]

             (DON *and* CAROL *dismount the tandem.* CAROL *moves downstage.* DON *stays at the bike.*)

CAROL   That's gospel, that; we were bombing round Pisa like Meatloaf! He spoke no Italian, the hospital was closed, but he attracted a doctor, explained what I needed, told them to ring a consultant and got me an ECG, all within an hour. That was better than I'd got when Rob had paid for me to go private, ten years ago! Mind you, if he'd've come to your house at midnight, sweating in lycra, and told you to go and get a cardiologist, what would you have done?

DON   Two hours later we were back at the hotel; it was a quarter to four in the morning and neither of us could sleep.

             [LXQ] [SQ]

             (DON *enters with a glass of water for* CAROL *and strikes the wine and wine glass. There is a developing friendship between the two of them.*)

CAROL   Probably a panic attack, he said! Tiredness and my age.

DON   Stress, and alcohol.

             (*A beat.*)

CAROL	I mean, I've never thought of myself as old, but . . .
DON	Well you're not old, are you?
CAROL	Well, I'm no spring chicken, though, am I?
DON	Well no, I don't suppose you are. (DON *grabs an apple from on set, and begins to eat it.*) Do you want an apple?
	(*A beat.*)
CAROL	No, thanks. (*A beat.*) I think it was brought on by you going on about Brexit!
DON	You brought it up!
	(*A beat.*)
CAROL	I thought you were joking when you said to get on the bike!
	(*A beat.*)
DON	Well we can scrap the bucket list if you want.
CAROL	You what, after what you've put me through? (*A beat.*) You'd have to take me back in a box.
	(*A beat.*)
DON	I thought I was going to have to!
CAROL	Well I've thought that you've been trying to kill me all there way down here, so . . .
DON	How come?
CAROL	Well, trying to keep up with you on that tandem; I've only got short legs, you know. Haven't you spotted that?

DON   So one question about this Brexit thing, rate . . .

               (*A beat.*)

CAROL   Oh no, you believed the 'multi-millionaire'
               men of the people, when they've let you down
               at every turn! You've voted for isolation, Don,
               when you've been on your own for eight years.
               You voted for an unstable world, and now
               you've got to watch it unfold! Coz where are we
               going to make up the forty-four percent of trade
               from? And what about the three million jobs
               we'll lose? And that's before I get to the art,
               and the universities and the research, and the
               border controls and the future for all our young
               people! They never expected to come out, you
               know, and now there'll be a horrible feeling of
               panic, because there's not a Plan B!

DON   Well they'll deliver on the NHS, I'll tell you
               that, because nobody could promise that and
               not deliver it.

CAROL   It'll be forgotten and never mentioned.

DON   No, it won't!

CAROL   We'll see!

DON   You're wrong!

CAROL   Well . . .

DON   People'll go bloody mad, Carol, if that happens.

               (CAROL *laughs involuntarily.*)

CAROL   It's politics, Don; you try and grab it and it
               disappears.

DON   I'm telling you!

CAROL   You're wrong!

DON   I don't think so.

            (DON *starts to eat the apple and* CAROL *finds him intriguing.*)

            What's up now?

CAROL   Nothing!

            (DON *devours the apple.*)

DON   Just the way you're looking . . .

CAROL   No, nothing.

DON   Nice!

CAROL   I thought it must be.

            (DON *eats the apple.*)

DON   It's only thing we've got, isn't it, NHS? NHS and Shakespeare, it's what we're known for. There'll be global embarrassment if they don't shell that money out.

CAROL   Looks like you're enjoying that, anyway?

DON   Oh, I like an apple. Jean used to say I ate 'em like a gorilla!

CAROL   Did she?

            (DON *references the apples behind the counter.*)

DON   There's a boatload there, if tha' wants one.

CAROL   Not bothered now, thanks!

DON   Well if you're feeling alight, Carol, I'm gunna try and get at least one good night's sleep. 'Night!

CAROL   Yes, 'night!

(DON *exits to become* ROB. *The sound of cicadas can be heard.* CAROL *has a moment and pours herself a glass of wine. As she does,* ROB *appears, caught in a vertical spotlight.*)

ROB   I told you not to take him with you!

CAROL   It must have been the teacher in me.

ROB   You can't save everybody, Carol!

CAROL   Do you know what, though? He's actually a nice guy.

ROB   They can't help but lash out and punch you in the face, though, can they?

CAROL   Well, I'd like to do that sometimes. Wouldn't you?

ROB   Sometimes!

CAROL   He wants to believe that those in power have his best interests at heart; it's never dawned on him that they just want to stay in power.

ROB   Bloody hell!

CAROL   But he is right about one thing, though: it's in danger of becoming a circus!

ROB   Oh yes, we'll be out, but we'll be in. We'll be in, but we'll be out. It'll be like you are all doing the Hokey Cokey!

(ROB *laughs and in a moment he has gone.*)

CAROL   We had one day in Florence, and to be honest, by then we were both completely exhausted, and I began to realise why they call it a bucket list. Well for a start, it was one of the few things that I could actually sit on!

[LXQ] [SQ]

(DON *and* CAROL *have made their way to the bikes on either side of the stage. They mount them and start to pedal easily. Gobos pick them out, and there is a sense of calm about them both; they call easily to each other as they make their way through Florence.*)

CAROL   That's the best of humanity, don't you think?

DON   Michelangelo's David! Never seen owt like it!

CAROL   Very honest.

DON   How is it?

CAROL   Well he did it with just a hammer and a chisel, for a start.

DON   Give over!

CAROL   Didn't you know?

DON   How old was he?

CAROL   Twenty-six, when he started it.

DON   The bloody scale of it!

CAROL   It makes you feel small, don't you think?

DON   David and Goliath: another unequal battle.

CAROL   You sort of forget that, don't you?

DON   I've always had sympathy for t' underdog, you know!

CAROL   Why's that, then?

DON   Coz I am one!

(*A beat.*)

CAROL   Every time I see it, it reminds me why I gave up
         art.

DON   Why's that?

CAROL   Because I was rubbish!

DON   Everybody's rubbish compared to that?

CAROL   Yes, but I sometimes wish that I'd've
         persevered. Too late now.

DON   Give over; it's never too late. Why can't you
         start doing it now?

CAROL   Because of my age. Who'd want my art?
         Nobody wants me at my age, Don. I can't see
         anybody wanting my artwork.

DON   You want it, don't you? Just do it for yourself;
         doesn't matter what anybody else thinks.
         Bollocks to 'em; just do it for yoursen if it makes
         you happy!

         (*A beat.*)

CAROL   I'm glad we're not cycling back. Are you?

DON   Give up; you'd walk it!

CAROL   It might have been easier; my behind is killing
         me!

DON   So is mine!

CAROL   You never said.

DON   Battle of wills, Carol.

CAROL   Is that what it's been?

DON	Very nearly!
	(*They laugh together easily.*)
CAROL	Well I can tick this one off, now!
DON	Yes, well straight back to work for me.
CAROL	How many days do you do?
DON	Some weeks I do three days. I'm on a rota, and I've got my retirement coming up and I don't fancy that. I will be lost, then. (*A beat.*) What are you gunna do?
CAROL	Well, I want to see if they're still setting the bins on fire, for a start. The police have been around, apparently.
DON	Have a word with 'em!
CAROL	They just laugh at me.
DON	That's what I'd do!
CAROL	I think that you might be a bit more persuasive than me, though!
DON	Yes, fair; I am good with people. Jean always said that. If ever there was a problem she'd send me out. Never keep a dog and bark yourself, she'd say . . . (DON *is struck by a sudden melancholy.*) And, I miss her, you know . . . I really miss her!
CAROL	I know what you mean.
DON	And I can't hear her voice so much down here. Isn't that weird?
	(*They pedal on easily.*)

CAROL   Thanks, you know, for coming.

DON   Well it wa' t' only offer I've had in nearly seven
               years, Carol, so I wasn't likely to turn it down,
               was I?

CAROL   You really know how to make a girl feel special,
               you know that, Don, don't you?

DON   Oh aye, I know that!

               (*They share a laugh together.*)

               [LXQ] [SQ]

               (CAROL *dismounts the bike and goes to her
               opening position, picking up the brush.* DON
               returns to mend his bike.)

CAROL   Over three years ago, that was. When we got
               back, I didn't see him for about two months,
               no texts, nothing! To be honest, it felt a bit
               strange; I mean we had been so close, and then
               nothing. It was like being a teenager again,
               the familiarity, the tit for tat, the company, if
               I'm honest. Just that. (*A beat.*) And I began to
               wonder if he was alright. So I texted him, and
               asked if he fancied a bike ride and a coffee.

               (DON *works on his bike.*)

DON   I wa' back at Ponte then, watching people
               struggle, watching a system failing under
               the weight of demand, watching an ageing
               population put trust in anybody who wore that
               badge. (*A beat.*) And does tha' know what?
               And this is rate, this is. There wasn't a day that
               went by when I didn't cry, I'll admit to that! (*A
               beat.*) There wasn't a day when I didn't have
               tears in my eyes over what has happened and
               how those people deserve better. That's what I

thought to be rate, does tha' know what? . . . The
people deserve better. Better bloody everything!

(CAROL *sweeps.* DON *works on his bike.*)

CAROL   And do you know what?

DON   Go on, what?

CAROL   Now, I agree with you on that!

DON   Well that's a bloody first!

            (DON *at the bike.*)

CAROL   And, you know, since Don's been up here fixing
            the bikes, and doing a bit of pottering for me,
            the kids haven't hung about round the back,
            and I've had no fires in the dustbins. In fact, I've
            had no security troubles at all.

DON   Yes well, I just had a word wi' em!

            (*A beat.*)

CAROL   Yes well, and I mean he's a bit scary for
            the punters sometimes, but you can't have
            everything, can you? (*She sweeps.*) And Brexit?

DON   Oph, don't!

CAROL   Where as it left us? Split down the middle! Deal
            or no deal? I can't remember voting for that,
            and I mean, I voted remain, and it kills me,
            because I've got to respect that we voted to
            leave. That's what you do in a democracy.

DON   It's not a democracy!

CAROL   We're like this all the time now!

DON   It's t' establishment looking after itself. People
               voted for sommat t' politicians didn't want,
               and they've done everything they could do to
               change it; even I realise that!

CAROL   But he's finally begun to realise that I was right;
               they were never going to give that money to the
               NHS, were they?

DON   Don't!

CAROL   They've even denied ever saying it, Don!

DON   I saw the bus; I saw it written with my own
               eyes! I followed the sod on my bloody bike!

CAROL   That means nothing these days!

DON   I mean, where do we go from here? Because I'm
               fucked if I know!

               (*A beat.*)

CAROL   He keeps saying that he's going to do something
               about it.

               (*A beat.*)

DON   I'd march, I'd take to the streets, but I just don't
               know who to believe in anymore! (*A beat.*) To
               be honest, I don't know what any of us can do.
               They've ruined the trust we put in 'em, and to
               me that's everything!

CAROL   Well, I know what you can do.

               (*A beat.*)

DON   What's that then?

               (*A beat.*)

CAROL   You can give me that fifty quid!

                 (CAROL *sweeps and* DON *mends the bikes as the music swells and the lights fade to blackout.*)

                 (*CURTAIN.*)